To: _____

From: _____

When someone does a kindness
It always seems to me
That's the way God up in heaven
Would like us all to be . . .

For when we bring some pleasure
To another human heart,
We have followed in His footsteps
And we've had a little part

In serving Him who loves us —
For I am very sure it's true
That in serving those around us
We serve and please Him, too.

Helen Steiner Rice

THE HELEN STEINER RICE FOUNDATION

Whatever the celebration, whatever the day, whatever the event, whatever the occasion, Helen Steiner Rice possessed the ability to express the appropriate feeling for that particular moment in time.

A happening became happier, a sentiment more sentimental, a memory more memorable because of her deep sensitivity to put into understandable language the emotion being experienced. Her positive attitude, her concern for others, and her love of God are identifiable threads woven into her life, her work . . . and even her death.

Prior to Mrs. Rice's passing, she established the HELEN STEINER RICE FOUNDATION, a nonprofit corporation whose purpose is to award grants to worthy charitable programs that assist the elderly and the needy.

Royalties from the sale of this book will add to the financial capabilities of the HELEN STEINER RICE FOUNDATION. Because of limited resources, the foundation presently limits grants to qualified charitable programs in Lorain, Ohio, where Helen Steiner Rice was born, and Greater Cincinnati, Ohio, where Mrs. Rice lived and worked most of her life. Hopefully, in the near future, resources will be of sufficient size that broader areas can be considered for the awarding of grants.

Because of her foresight, caring, and deep conviction of sharing, Helen Steiner Rice continues to touch a countless number of lives through grants and through her inspirational poetry.

Helen Steiner Rice

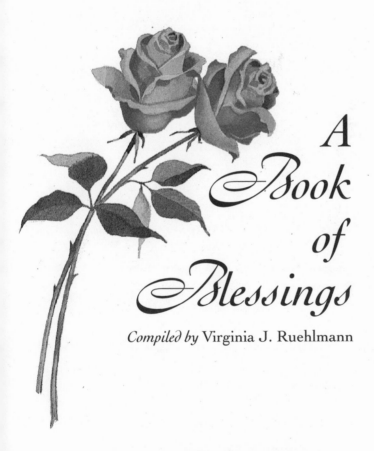

A

Book

of

Blessings

Compiled by Virginia J. Ruehlmann

Fleming H. Revell
A Division of Baker Book House Co
Grand Rapids, Michigan 49516

Published by Fleming H. Revell
a division of Baker Book House Company
P.O. Box 6287, Grand Rapids, MI 49516-6287

Third printing, March 1996

Printed in the United States of America

ISBN 0-8007-1714-7

Jacket and interior illustrations by Jack Brouwer

Scripture quotations marked RSV are taken from the Revised Standard Version of the
Bible, copyright 1946, 1952, 1971, and 1973 by the Division of Christian Education of
the National Council of the Churches of Christ in the United States of America.

Scripture verses marked NIV are taken from the HOLY BIBLE, NEW
INTERNATIONAL VERSION ®. NIV®. Copyright © 1973, 1978, 1984, by
International Bible Society. Used by permission of Zondervan Publishing House. All
rights reserved.

Scripture selections from the New American Bible (NAB) Copyright © 1970 by the
Confraternity of Christian Doctrine, Washington, D.C., are used with permission. All
rights reserved.

Lovingly I dedicate
    each thought herein expressed
To all who read this little book,
    and may their lives be blessed . . .
For only warm, responsive hearts
    and God's guidance from above
Could fill these lines with meaning
    and with hope and faith and love.

My foot stands on level ground; in the great congregation I will bless the Lord.

Psalm 26:12 RSV

Contents

Introduction

Wishing God's sweet blessings
Not in droplets but a shower,
To fall on you throughout the day
And brighten every hour.

A pilgrimage to the Holy Land increases one's faith, inspirations, and amazement. Visiting Capernaum and the Sea of Galilee sparks an incredible realization that the visitor is perhaps walking the same path that Jesus traveled when He delivered the Sermon on the Mount. His words in that sermon startled the crowd and challenged the basic attitudes and values of that day—and the present!

Envision Jesus climbing the mountainside with the crowd following, finding a level spot, and sitting down to teach, as was the custom then for rabbis. The listeners were amazed at His message.

The Beatitudes promise that many blessings are available when we live our individual lives in a fashion that is pleasing to God and when we concentrate on important Christian values rather than unimportant worldly aspects.

If Jesus were to deliver His Sermon on the Mount today, our secular world would again be startled. The lessons in the Beatitudes are equally important and timely in the here and now as in the day when spoken originally by Jesus. His principles stressed a lifestyle of agape love, charity, forgiveness, humility, trust, and a dependence upon God rather than the worldly goals of wealth, pleasure, and self-justification.

Helen Steiner Rice endeavored to live by the philosophy espoused by Jesus. Her poetry vividly, effectively, and inspirationally expresses the same spiritual concepts and values that are inherent in the message of the Beatitudes.

May *A Book of Blessings* be a blessing in your life and, by your example and actions, may your life be a blessing to others. Permit God's love to flow through you.

May God's choicest blessings be yours.

Virginia J. Ruehlmann

*Blessed are
the poor in spirit,
for theirs is the kingdom
of heaven.*

Matthew 5:3 NIV

Blessings without End

Put Your Problems in God's Hands

Although it sometimes seems to us
   our prayers have not been heard,
God always knows our every need
   without a single word,
And He will not forsake us
   even though the way is steep,
For He is always near to us,
   a tender watch to keep . . .
And in good time He'll answer us,
   and in His love He'll send
Greater things than we have asked
   and blessings without end.
So though we do not understand
   why trouble comes to man,
Can we not be contented
   just to know it is God's plan?

Blessed are all who take refuge in him.
Psalm 2:12 RSV

A Child's Prayer

Hear me, blessed Jesus,
   as I say my prayers today.
Tell me You are close to me
   and You'll never go away.
Tell me that You love me
   like the Bible says You do,
And tell me also, Jesus,
   I can always come to You,
And You will understand me
   when other people don't,
And though some may forget me,
   just tell me that You won't . . .
And someday when I'm older,
   I will show You it is true
That even as a little child
   my heart belongs to You.

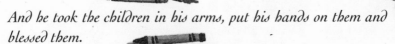

And he took the children in his arms, put his hands on them and blessed them.

Mark 10:16 NIV

Blessings in Disguise

God sends His little angels
    in many forms and guises.
They come as lovely miracles
    that God alone devises,
For He does nothing without purpose —
    everything's a perfect plan
To fulfill in bounteous measure
    all He ever promised and . . .
Every little angel
    with a body bent and broken

Or a little mind unknowing
  or little words unspoken
Is just God's way of trying
  to reach out and touch the hands
Of all who do not know Him
  and cannot understand
That often through an angel
  whose wings will never fly
The Lord is pointing out
  the way to His eternal sky,
Where there will be no handicaps
  of body, soul, or mind,
And where all limitations
  will be dropped and left behind . . .
So accept these little angels
  as gifts from God above,
And thank Him for this lesson
  in faith and hope and love.

You shall serve the Lord your God, and I will bless your bread and your water; and I will take sickness away from the midst of you.

Exodus 23:25 RSV

God Keep You in His Care

There are many things in life
 we cannot understand,
But we must trust God's judgment
 and be guided by His hand . . .

And all who have God's blessing
 can rest safely in His care,
For He promises safe passage
 on the wings of faith and prayer.

*O save thy people, and bless thy heritage: be thou their shepherd,
and carry them for ever.*

Psalm 28:9 RSV

God's Sweetest Appointments

Out of life's misery born of man's sins,
A fuller, richer life begins,
For when we are helpless with no place to go
And our hearts are heavy and our spirits are low,
If we place our lives in God's hands
And surrender completely to His will and demands,
The darkness lifts and the sun shines through,
And by His touch we are born anew.
So praise God for trouble that cuts like a knife
And disappointments that shatter your life,
For with patience to wait and faith to endure,
Your life will be blessed and your future secure,
For God is but testing your faith and your love
Before He appoints you to rise far above
All the small things that so sorely distress you,
For God's only intention is to strengthen and bless you.

Blessed are those who have learned to acclaim you, who walk in the light of your presence, O Lord.

Psalm 89:15 NIV

*L*ive by Faith and *N*ot by Feelings

When everything is pleasant and bright
And the things we do turn out just right,
We feel without question that God is real,
For when we are happy, how good we feel,
But when the tides turn and gone is the song
And misfortune comes and our plans go wrong,
Doubt creeps in and we start to wonder
And our thoughts about God are torn asunder—
For we feel deserted in times of deep stress
Without God's presence to assure us and bless,
And it is when our senses are reeling
We realize clearly it's faith and not feeling,
For it takes great faith to patiently wait,
Believing God comes not too soon or too late.

A faithful man will be richly blessed.
Proverbs 28:20 NIV

Blessed are those who mourn, for they will be comforted.

Matthew 5:4 NIV

Blessings in Times of Trial

Count Your Gains and Not Your Losses

As we travel down life's busy road
Complaining of our heavy load,
We often think God's been unfair
And gave us much more than our share
Of daily little irritations
And disappointing tribulations.

We're discontented with our lot
And all the bad breaks that we got.
We count our losses not our gain,
And remember only tears and pain.
The good things we forget completely—
When God looked down and blessed us sweetly.

Our troubles fill our every thought—
We dwell upon the goals we sought
And, wrapped up in our own despair,
We have no time to see or share
Another's load that far outweighs
Our little problems and dismays.

And so we walk with heads held low,
And little do we guess or know
That someone near us on life's street
Is burdened deeply with defeat,
And if we'd but forget our care
And stop in sympathy to share
The burden that our brother carried,
Our minds and hearts would be less harried
And we would feel our load was small—
In fact, we carried no load at all.

When you reap your harvest in your field, and have forgotten a sheaf in the field, you shall not go back to get it; it shall be for the sojourner, the fatherless, and the widow; that the Lord your God may bless you in all the work of your hands.

Deuteronomy 24:19 RSV

I Said a Special Prayer for You

I said a birthday prayer for you
and I asked the Lord above
To keep you safely in His care
and enfold you in His love.
I did not ask for fortune,
for riches or for fame —
I only asked for blessings
in the Savior's holy name —
Blessings to surround you
in times of trial and stress,
And inner joy to fill your heart
with peace and happiness.

*May the Lord give strength to his people! May the Lord
bless his people with peace!*

Psalm 29:11 RSV

The Blessing of Sharing

Only what we give away
Enriches us from day to day,
For not in getting but in giving
Is found the lasting joy of living,
For no one ever had a part
In sharing treasures of the heart
Who did not feel the impact of
The magic mystery of God's love.
Love alone can make us kind
And give us joy and peace of mind,
So live with joy unselfishly
And you'll be blessed abundantly.

Blessed are they who maintain justice, who constantly do what is right.

Psalm 106:3 NIV

A Time of Renewal

No one likes to be sick
    and yet we know
It takes sunshine and rain
    to make flowers grow . . .
And if we never were sick
    and we never felt pain,
We'd be like a desert
    without any rain . . .
And who wants a life
    that is barren and dry,
With never a cloud
    to darken the sky?
For continuous sun
    goes unrecognized
Like the blessings God sends,
    which are often disguised,
For sometimes a sickness
    that seems so distressing
Is a time of renewal
    and spiritual blessing.

The king will say to those on his right: "Come, you have my Father's blessing!"

Matthew 25:34 NAB

No Room for Blessings

Refuse to be discouraged—
   refuse to be distressed,
For when we are despondent,
   our lives cannot be blessed.
Doubt and fear and worry
   close the door to faith and prayer,
And there's no room for blessings
   when we're lost in deep despair.
So remember when you're troubled
   with uncertainty and doubt,
It is best to tell our Father
   what our fear is all about.
For unless we seek His guidance
   when troubled times arise,
We are bound to make decisions
   that are twisted and unwise.
But when we view our problems
   through the eyes of God above,
Misfortunes turn to blessings
   and hatred turns to love.

Blessed by God, because he has not rejected my prayer or removed his steadfast love from me!

Psalm 66:20 RSV

The Blessings
of Patience and Comfort

Realizing my helplessness,
I'm asking God if He will bless
The thoughts you think and all you do
So these dark hours you're passing through
Will lose their grave anxiety
And only deep tranquillity
Will fill your mind and help impart
New strength and courage to your heart.

So take the Savior's loving hand
And do not try to understand—
Just let Him lead you where He will,
Through pastures green and waters still,
And though the way ahead seems steep,
Be not afraid for He will keep
Tender watch through night and day,
And He will hear each prayer you pray.

So place yourself in His loving care
And He will gladly help you bear
Whatever lies ahead of you
For there is nothing God can't do . . .
So I commend you into God's care,
And each day I will say a prayer
That you will feel His presence near
To help dissolve your every fear.

Blessed are all those who wait for him.
Isaiah 30:18 RSV

Blessed are the meek, for they will inherit the earth.
Matthew 5:5 NIV

*O*pen Your Heart
to Blessings

My Prayer

Bless me, heavenly Father —
  forgive my erring ways.
Grant me strength to serve Thee,
  put purpose in my days.
Give me understanding,
  enough to make me kind,
So I may judge all people
  with my heart and not my mind.
Teach me to be patient
  in everything I do,
Content to trust Your wisdom
  and to follow after You.
Help me when I falter
  and hear me when I pray,
And receive me in Thy kingdom
  to dwell with Thee someday.

O Lord Almighty, blessed is the man who trusts in you.
Psalm 84:12 NIV

Blessed Little Memories

Tender little memories
of little things we've done
Make the very darkest day
a bright and happy one.
Tender little memories
of some word or deed
Give us strength and courage
when we are in need.
Blessed little memories
help us bear the cross
And soften all the bitterness
of failure and of loss.
Priceless little memories
are treasures you can't buy,
And oh, how poor the world is
compared to you and I.

Blessed is he who comes in the name of the Lord. From the house of the Lord we bless you.

Psalm 118:26 NIV

Open the Door to Blessings

Father, make us kind and wise
So we may always recognize
The blessings that are ours to take,
The friendships that are ours to make,
If we but open our heart's door wide
To let the sunshine of love inside.

*Sing to the Lord, bless his name; tell of his salvation
from day to day.*

Psalm 96:2 RSV

God's Keeping

To be in God's keeping
　　is surely a blessing,
For, though life is often
　　dark and distressing,
No day is too dark
　　and no burden too great
That God in His love
　　cannot penetrate . . .
And to know and believe
　　without question or doubt
That no matter what happens
　　God is there to help out
Is to hold in your hand
　　the golden key
To peace and joy
　　and serenity.

Bless the Lord, O my soul! O Lord my God, thou art very great!
Psalm 104:1 RSV

Is the Cross You Wear Too Heavy to Bear?

Complainingly I told myself
  this cross was too heavy to wear,
And I wondered discontentedly
  why God gave it to me to bear.
I looked with envy at others
  whose crosses seemed lighter than mine
And wished that I could change my cross
  for one of a lighter design.

Then in a dream I beheld the cross
  I impulsively wanted to wear —
It was fashioned of pearls and diamonds
  and gems that are precious and rare,
And when I hung it around my neck,
  the weight of the jewels and the gold
Was much too heavy and cumbersome
  for my small, slender neck to hold.

So I tossed it aside, and before my eyes
  was a cross of rose-red flowers,
And I said with delight as I put it on,
  "This cross I can wear for hours."

For it was so dainty and fragile,
    so lovely and light and thin,
But I had forgotten about the thorns
    that started to pierce my skin.

Then in a dream I saw my cross —
    rugged and old and plain —
The clumsy old cross I had looked upon
    with discontented disdain,
And at last I knew that God had made
    this special cross for me,
For God in His great wisdom
    knew what I before could not see —
That often the loveliest crosses
    are the heaviest crosses to bear,
For only God is wise enough
    to choose the cross each can wear.

So never complain about your cross,
    for your cross has been blessed —
God made it just for you to wear
    and remember, God knows best.

This blessing has fallen to me, that I have kept thy precepts.
Psalm 119:56 RSV

Look on the Sunny Side

There are always two sides —
  the good and the bad,
The dark and the light,
  the sad and the glad —
But in looking back over
  the good and the bad,
We're aware of the number
  of good things we've had,
And in counting our blessings,
  we find when we're through
We've no reason at all
  to complain or be blue.

So thank God for good things
   He's already done,
And be grateful to Him
   for the battles you've won,
And know that the same God
   who helped you before
Is ready and willing
   to help once more.
Then with faith in your heart,
   reach out for God's hand
And accept what He sends,
   though you can't understand . . .
For our Father in heaven
   always knows what is best,
And if you trust His wisdom,
   your life will be blessed . . .
For always remember that
   whatever betide you,
You are never alone,
   for God is beside you.

The Autumn of Life

What a wonderful time is life's autumn,
    when the leaves of the trees are all gold,
When God fills each day as He sends it
    with memories, priceless and old.
What a treasure-house filled with rare jewels
    are the blessings of year upon year,
When life has been lived as you've lived it
    in a home where God's presence is near . . .
May the deep meaning surrounding this day,
    like the paintbrush of God up above,
Touch your life with wonderful blessings
    and fill your heart brimful with His love.

Amen! Blessing and glory and wisdom and thanksgiving and honor and power and might be to our God for ever and ever! Amen.
Revelation 7:12 RSV

Blessed are those who hunger and thirst for righteousness, for they will be filled.

Matthew 5:6 NIV

$\mathcal{B}$lessings
for All Seasons

How to Find Happiness

Happiness is something you create in your mind,
Not something you search for but can't seem to find,
Not something that's purchased with silver or gold,
Not something that force can capture and hold.
It's just waking up and beginning each day
By counting your blessings and kneeling to pray.
It's giving up thoughts that breed discontent
And accepting what comes as a gift heaven-sent.
It's giving up wishing for things you have not
And making the best of whatever you've got.
It's knowing that life is determined and planned
And God holds the world in the palm of His hand.
And it's by completing what God gives you to do
That you find contentment and happiness, too.

Blessed are they whose ways are blameless, who walk according to the law of the Lord.

Psalm 119:1 NIV

My Birthday in the Hospital

How little we know what God has in store
As daily He blesses our lives more and more.
I've lived many years and I've learned many things,
But today I have grown new spiritual wings . . .
For pain has a way of broadening our view
And bringing us closer in sympathy, too,
To those who are living in constant pain
And trying somehow to bravely sustain
The faith and endurance to keep on trying
When they almost welcome the peace of dying . . .
Without this experience I would have lived and died
Without fathoming the pain of Christ crucified,
For none of us knows what pain is all about
Until our spiritual wings start to sprout.
So thank You, God, for the gift You sent
To teach me that pain's heaven-sent.

Blessed is he who has regard for the weak; the Lord delivers him in times of trouble.

Psalm 41:1 NIV

Daily Prayers
Dissolve Your Cares

I meet God in the morning
   and go with Him through the day,
Then in the stillness of the night
   before sleep comes I pray
That God will just take over
   all the problems I couldn't solve,
And in the peacefulness of sleep
   my cares will all dissolve.
So when I open up my eyes
   to greet another day,
I'll find myself renewed in strength
   and there will open up a way
To meet what seemed impossible
   for me to solve alone,
And once again I'll be assured
   I am never on my own.
For if we try to stand alone,
   we are weak and we will fall,
For God is always greatest
   when we're helpless, lost, and small.

And no day is unmeetable
    if, on rising, our first thought
Is to thank God for the blessings
    that His loving care has brought . . .
For there can be no failures
    or hopeless, unsaved sinners
If we enlist the help of God,
    who makes all losers winners.

So meet Him in the morning
    and go with Him through the day,
And thank Him for His guidance
    each evening when you pray—
And if you follow faithfully
    this daily way to pray,
You will never in your lifetime
    face another hopeless day.

You also must help us by prayer, so that many will give thanks on
our behalf for the blessing granted us in answer to many prayers.
2 Corinthians 1:11 RSV

Learn to Rest

We all need short vacations
   in life's fast and maddening race—
An interlude of quietness
   from the constant, jet-age pace.
So when your day is pressure-packed
   and your hours are all too few,
Just close your eyes and meditate
   and let God talk to you . . .

For when we keep on pushing,
    we're not following in God's way—
We are foolish, selfish robots
    mechanized to fill each day
With unimportant trivia
    that makes life more complex
And gives us greater problems
    to irritate and vex
So when your nervous network
    becomes a tangled mess,
Just close your eyes in silent prayer
    and ask the Lord to bless
Each thought that you are thinking,
    each decision you must make,
As well as every word you speak
    and every step you take—
For only by the grace of God
    can you gain self-control,
And only meditative thoughts
    can restore your peace of soul.

But blest are your eyes because they see and blest are your ears because they hear.

Matthew 13:16 NAB

The Seasons of the Soul

Why am I cast down and despondently sad
When I long to be happy and joyous and glad?
Why is my heart heavy with unbearable weight
As I try to escape this soul-saddened state?
I ask myself often what makes life this way —
Why is the song silenced in my heart today?
And then with God's help it all becomes clear —

The soul has its seasons just the same as the year.
I too must pass through life's autumn of dying,
A desolate period of heart-hurt and crying,
Followed by winter, in whose frostbitten hand
My heart is as frozen as the snow-covered land.
We too must pass through the seasons God sends,
Content in the knowledge that everything ends.

Praise the Lord. Blessed is the man who fears the Lord, who finds great delight in his commands.

Psalm 112:1 NIV

Blessed are the merciful, for they will be shown mercy.
Matthew 5:7 NIV

Showers of Blessings

Showers of Blessings

Each day there are showers of blessings
   sent from the Father above,
For God is a great, lavish giver,
   and there is no end to His love . . .
And His grace is more than sufficient,
   His mercy is boundless and deep,
And His infinite blessings are countless —
   and all this we're given to keep
If we but seek God and find Him
   and ask for a bounteous measure
Of this wholly immeasurable offering
   from God's inexhaustible treasure . . .

For no matter how big man's dreams are,
God's blessings are infinitely more,
For always God's giving is greater
than what man is asking for.

I will send down showers in season; there will be showers of blessings.
Ezekiel 34:26 NIV

Blessings Devised by God

God speaks to us in many ways,
Altering our lives, our plans and days,
And His blessings come in many guises
That He alone in love devises,
And sorrow, which we dread so much,
Can bring a very healing touch . . .
For when we fail to heed His voice
We leave the Lord no other choice
Except to use a firm, stern hand
To make us know He's in command . . .
For on the wings of loss and pain,
The peace we often sought in vain
Will come to us with sweet surprise,
For God is merciful and wise . . .
And through dark hours of tribulation
God gives us time for meditation,
And nothing can be counted loss
Which teaches us to bear our cross.

Every day I will bless thee, and praise thy name for ever and ever.
Psalm 145:2 RSV

You Too Must Weep

Let me not live a life that's free
From the things that draw me close to Thee,
For how can I ever hope to heal
The wounds of others I do not feel?
If my eyes are dry and I never weep,
How do I know when the hurt is deep?
If my heart is cold and it never bleeds,
How can I tell what my brother needs?

For when ears are deaf to the beggar's plea
And we close our eyes and refuse to see
And we steel our hearts and harden our minds
And we count it a weakness whenever we're kind,
We are no longer following the Father's way
Or seeking His guidance from day to day.

For, without crosses to carry and burdens to bear,
We dance through a life that is frothy and fair,
And, chasing the rainbow, we have no desire
For roads that are rough and realms that are higher.

So spare me no heartache or sorrow, dear Lord,
For the heart that hurts reaps the richest reward,
And God blesses the heart that is broken with sorrow
As He opens the door to a brighter tomorrow.
For only through tears can we recognize
The suffering that lies in another's eyes.

Yet our God turned the curse into a blessing.
Nehemiah 13:2 RSV

God So Loved the World

Our Father up in heaven,
  long, long years ago,
Looked down in His great mercy
  upon the earth below
And saw that folks were lonely
  and lost in deep despair,
And so He said, "I'll send My Son
  to walk among them there
So they can hear Him speaking
  and feel His nearness, too,
And see the many miracles
  that faith alone can do,

For I know it will be easier
　　to believe and understand
If man can see and talk to Him
　　and touch His healing hand."

So whenever we have troubles
　　and we're overcome by cares,
We can take it all to Jesus,
　　for He understands our prayers.
For He too lived and suffered
　　in a world much like our own,
And no man can know the sorrow
　　that Jesus Christ has known.

And whatever we endure on earth
　　is so very, very small
When compared to God's beloved Son
　　who was sent to save us all.
And the blessed reassurance
　　that He lived much as we do
Is a source of strength and comfort,
　　and it gives us courage, too.

Blessed are all who fear the Lord, who walk in his ways.
Psalm 128:1 NIV

A Thankful Heart

Take nothing for granted,
   for whenever you do,
The joy of enjoying
   is lessened for you.
For we rob our own lives
   much more than we know
When we fail to respond
   or in any way show
Our thanks for the blessings
   that daily are ours —
The warmth of the sun,
   the fragrance of flowers,
The beauty of twilight,
   the freshness of dawn,
The coolness of dew
   on a green velvet lawn,
The kind little deeds
   so thoughtfully done,
The favors of friends
   and the love that someone
Unselfishly gives us
   in a myriad of ways,
Expecting no payment
   and no words of praise.

Oh, great is our loss
 when we no longer find
A thankful response
 to things of this kind,
For the joy of enjoying
 and the fullness of living
Are found in the heart
 that is filled with thanksgiving.

For seven days you shall keep the feast to the Lord your God at the place which the Lord will choose; because the Lord your God will bless you in all your produce and in all the work of your hands, so that you will be altogether joyful.

Deuteronomy 16:15 RSV

Thank You, God, for Everything

Thank You, God, for everything—
   the big things and the small—
For every good gift comes from God,
   the Giver of them all,
And all too often we accept
   without any thanks or praise
The gifts God sends as blessings
   each day in many ways.

First, thank You for the little things
    that often come our way—
The things we take for granted
    and don't mention when we pray—
The unexpected courtesy,
    the thoughtful, kindly deed,
A hand reached out to help us
    in the time of sudden need.

Oh, make us more aware, dear God,
    of little daily graces
That come to us with sweet surprise
    from never-dreamed-of places.
Then thank You for the miracles
    we are much too blind to see,
And give us new awareness
    of our many gifts from Thee . . .
And help us to remember
    that the key to life and living
Is to make each prayer a prayer of thanks
    and every day Thanksgiving.

The Lord will command the blessing upon you in your barns, and in all that you undertake; and he will bless you in the land which the Lord your God gives you.

Deuteronomy 28:8 RSV

Blessed are the pure in heart, for they will see God.
Matthew 5:8 NIV

Be Glad
for God's Blessings

What Is a Blessing?

The good, green earth beneath your feet,
The air you breathe, the food you eat,
Some work to do, a goal to win,
A sense of peace deep down within—
In these simple things may you always find
Joys of the very greatest kind.

Bless the Lord, O my soul; and all that is within me, bless his holy name!

Psalm 103:1 RSV

Man Cannot Live by Bread Alone

He lived in a palace on a mountain of gold,
Surrounded by riches and wealth untold,
Priceless possessions and treasures of art,
But he died alone of a hungry heart,
For man cannot live by bread alone
No matter what he may have or own,
For though he reaches his earthly goal,
He'll waste away with a starving soul,
But he who eats of the holy bread
Will always find his spirit fed,
And even the poorest of men can afford
To feast at the table prepared by the Lord.

*Do, then, bless the house of your servant that it may be before you
forever; for you, Lord God, have promised, and by your blessing
the house of your servant shall be blessed forever.*

2 Samuel 7:29 NAB

ℬe Glad

Be glad that your life has been full and complete,
Be glad that you've tasted the bitter and sweet.
Be glad that you've walked in sunshine and rain,
Be glad that you've felt both pleasure and pain.
Be glad that you've had such a full, happy life,
Be glad for your joy as well as your strife.
Be glad that you've walked with courage each day,
Be glad you've had strength each step of the way.
Be glad for the comfort that you've found in prayer,
Be glad for God's blessings, His love, and His care.

Enter his gates with thanksgiving, and his courts with praise!
Give thanks to him, bless his name!

Psalm 100:4 RSV

Meet Life's Trials with Smiles

There are times when life overwhelms us
   and our trials seem too many to bear—
It is then we should stop to remember
   God is standing by ready to share
The uncertain hours that confront us
   and fill us with fear and despair,
For God in His goodness has promised
   that the cross that He gives us to wear
Will never exceed our endurance
   or be more than our strength can bear.
And secure in that blessed assurance,
   we can smile as we face tomorrow,
For God holds the key to the future,
   and no sorrow or care we need borrow.

Blessed be the God and Father of our Lord Jesus Christ, who has blessed us in Christ with every spiritual blessing in the heavenly places.

Ephesians 1:3 NAB

God, Give Us Drive

There's a difference between drive and driven —
The one is selfish, the other God-given,
For the driven man has but one goal —
Just worldly wealth and not riches of soul . . .
And daily he 's spurred on to reach and attain
A higher position, more profit and gain.
Ambition and wealth become his great needs
As daily he's driven by avarice and greed.

But most blessed are they who use their drive
To work with zeal so all men may survive,
For while they forfeit great personal gain,
Their work and their zeal are never in vain,
For they contribute to the whole human race,
And we cannot survive without growing in grace.

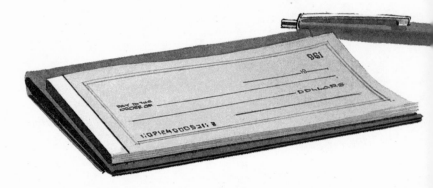

So help us, dear God, to choose between
The driving forces that rule our routine
So we may make our purpose and goal
Not power and wealth but the growth of our souls,
And give us strength and drive and desire
To raise our standards and ethics higher,
So all of us and not just a few
May live on earth as You want us to.

Him who monopolizes grain, the people curse — but blessings upon the head of him who distributes it!

Proverbs 11:26 NAB

Blessed are the peacemakers, for they will be called sons of God.

Matthew 5:9 NIV

Unfailing Blessings

The First Thing Every Morning and the Last Thing Every Night

Were you too busy this morning
   to quietly stop and pray?
Did you hurry and drink your coffee
   then frantically rush away,
Consoling yourself by saying—
   God will always be there
Waiting to hear my petitions,
   ready to answer each prayer?

It's true that the great, generous Savior
   forgives our transgressions each day
And patiently waits for lost sheep
   who constantly seem to stray,
But moments of prayer once omitted
   in the busy rush of the day
Can never again be recaptured,
   for they silently slip away.

Strength is gained in the morning
   to endure the trials of the day
When we visit with God in person
   in a quiet and unhurried way,
For only through prayer that's unhurried
   can the needs of the day be met
And only in prayers said at evening
   can we sleep without fears or regret.

For all of our errors and failures
   that we made in the course of the day
Are freely forgiven at nighttime
   when we kneel down and earnestly pray,
So seek the Lord in the morning
   and never forget Him at night,
For prayer is an unfailing blessing
   that makes every burden seem light.

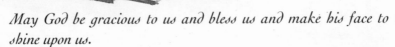

May God be gracious to us and bless us and make his face to shine upon us.

Psalm 67:1 RSV

God Gave Man the Earth

The earth is the Lord's, and the fullness thereof . . ."
He gave it to man as a gift of His love
So all men might live as He hoped they would,
Sharing together all things that were good,
But man only destroyed the good earth of God.
He polluted the air and ravished the sod,
He cut down the forests with ruthless disdain,
And the earth's natural beauty he perverted for gain.
And now in an age filled with violent dissent,
Man finds he's imprisoned in his own discontent.
He has taken the earth that God placed in his care
And built his own hell without being aware
That the future we face was fashioned by man,
Who in ignorance resisted God's beautiful plan,

And what God created to be paradise
Became by man's lust and perversion and vice
A cauldron of chaos in a fog of pollution
To which man can find no cure or solution.
How far man will go to complete his destruction
Is beyond a computer's robot deduction.

For land which has drunk the rain that often falls upon it, and brings forth vegetation useful to those for whose sake it is cultivated, receives a blessing from God.

Hebrews 6:7 RSV

Counting the Blessings

Nothing would make me happier
   or please me any better
Than to write you my thanks
   in a long, friendly letter,
For being remembered
   at the holiday season
By someone like you
   gave my heart ample reason
To count all my blessings,
   and your friendship is one —
For without fans and friends,
   all the writing I've done
Would lose all its meaning,
   its warmth and sincereness,

For how could I write
   without feeling a nearness
To all the dear people
   who interpret each line
With their own love and kindness,
   which become part of mine,
So, more than you know,
   I thank God above
For fans, friends, and family
   and their gifts of love.

You shall give to him freely, and your heart shall not be grudging when you give to him; because for this the Lord your God will bless you in all your work and in all that you undertake.

Deuteronomy 15:10 RSV

There Is a Reason for Everything

Our Father knows what's best for us,
  so why should we complain?
We always want the sunshine
  but He knows there must be rain.
We love the sound of laughter
  and the merriment of cheer,
But our hearts would lose their tenderness
  if we never shed a tear.

Our Father tests us often
  with suffering and with sorrow.
He tests us not to punish us
  but to help us meet tomorrow,
For growing trees are strengthened
  when they withstand the storm,
And the sharp cut of a chisel
  gives the marble grace and form.

God never hurts us needlessly
   and He never wastes our pain,
For every loss He sends to us
   is followed by rich gain,
And when we count the blessings
   that God has so freely sent,
We will find no cause for murmuring
   and no time to lament.

For our Father loves His children
   and to Him all things are plain,
He never sends us pleasure
   when the soul's deep need is pain.
So whenever we are troubled and
   when everything goes wrong,
It is just God working in us
   to make our spirits strong.

Blessed is the nation whose God is the Lord, the people he chose for his inheritance.

Psalm 33:12 NIV

Blessed are those who are persecuted because of righteousness, for theirs is the kingdom of heaven.

Matthew 5:10 NIV

Blessings amid Trouble

It Takes the Bitter and Sweet

Life is a mixture
   of sunshine and rain,
Laughter and teardrops,
   pleasure and pain,
Low tides and high tides,
   mountains and plains,
Triumphs, defeats,
   and losses and gains,
But always in all ways
   or some dread affliction,
Be assured that it comes
   with God's kind benediction,
And if we accept it
   as a gift of His love,
We'll be showered with blessings
   from our Father above.

Taste and see that the Lord is good; blessed is the man who takes refuge in him.

Psalm 34:8 NIV

God's Assurance Gives Us Endurance

My blessings are so many,
   my troubles are so few —
How can I be discouraged
   when I know that I have You?
And I have the sweet assurance
   that there's nothing I need fear
If I but keep remembering
   I am Yours and You are near,
Help me to endure the storms
   that keep raging deep inside me,
And make me more aware each day
   that no evil can betide me.
If I remain undaunted
   though the billows sweep and roll,
Knowing I have Your assurance,
   there's a haven for my soul,
For anything and everything
   can somehow be endured
If Your presence is beside me
   and lovingly assured.

Bless the Lord, O my soul, and forget not all his benefits.
Psalm 103:2 RSV

Adversity Can Bless Us

The way we use adversity
 is strictly our own choice,
For in God's hands
 adversity can make the heart rejoice.
For everything God sends to us,
 no matter in what form,
Is sent with plan and purpose,
 for by the fierceness of a storm
The atmosphere is changed and cleared
 and the earth is washed and clean,
And the high winds of adversity
 can make restless souls serene.

And while it's very difficult
   for mankind to understand
God's intentions and His purpose
   and the workings of His hand,
If we observe the miracles
   that happen every day,
We cannot help but be convinced
   that in His wondrous way
God makes what seemed unbearable
   and painful and distressing
Easily acceptable
   when we view it as a blessing.

The Lord will open to you his good treasury the heavens, to give the rain of your land in its season and to bless all the work of your hands.

Deuteronomy 28:12 RSV

Trouble Is a Steppingstone

Trouble is something no one can escape —
Everyone has it in some form or shape.
Some people hide it way down deep inside,
Some people bear it with gallant-like pride.
Some people worry and complain of their lot,
Some people covet what they haven't got
While others rebel and become bitter and old
With hopes that are dead and hearts that are cold.
But the wise man accepts whatever God sends,
Willing to yield like a storm-tossed tree bends,
Knowing that God never made a mistake,
So whatever He sends they are willing to take.

For trouble is part and parcel of life,
And no man can grow without struggle or strife,
The steep hills ahead and the high mountain peaks
Afford man at last the peace that he seeks . . .
So blessed are the people who learn to accept
The trouble men try to escape and reject,
For in our acceptance we're given great grace
And courage and faith and the strength to face
The daily troubles that come to us all,
So we may learn to stand straight and tall . . .
For the grandeur of life is born of defeat,
And in overcoming we make life complete.

We work hard with our own hands. When we are cursed, we bless; when we are persecuted, we endure it; when we are slandered, we answer kindly.

1 Corinthians 4:12–13 NIV

Priceless Treasures

What could I give you that would truly please
In topsy-turvy times like these?
I can't take away or even make less
The things that annoy, disturb, and distress,
For stores don't sell a single thing
To make the heart that's troubled sing.
They sell rare gifts that are ultra-smart
But nothing to warm or comfort the heart.
The joys of life that cheer and bless
The stores don't sell, I must confess,
But friends and prayers are priceless treasures
Beyond all monetary measures,
And so I say a special prayer
That God will keep you in His care,
And if I can ever help you, dear,
In any way throughout the year,
You've only to call, for as long as I live,
Such as I have I freely give.

I bless the Lord who gives me counsel; in the night also my heart instructs me.

Psalm 16:7 RSV

Blessings Come in Many Guises

When troubles come and things go wrong
And days are cheerless and nights are long,
We find it so easy to give in to despair
By magnifying the burdens we bear.
We add to our worries by refusing to try
To look for the rainbow in an overcast sky,
And the blessings God sent in a darkened disguise
Our troubled hearts failed to recognize,
Not knowing God sent it not to distress us
But to strengthen our faith and redeem and bless us.

Blessed is the man you discipline, O Lord: the man you teach from your law.

Psalm 94:12 NIV

Blessing of God's Seasons

We know we must pass
   through the seasons God sends,
Content in the knowledge
   that everything ends,
And, oh, what a blessing
   to know there are reasons
And to find that our souls
   must, too, have their seasons—
Bounteous seasons and barren ones, too,
   times for rejoicing and times to be blue—
But meeting these seasons of dark desolation
   with the strength that is born of anticipation
Comes from knowing that every season of sadness
   will surely be followed by a springtime of gladness.

*Blessed is the man who walks not in the counsel of the wicked, . . .
on his law he meditates day and night. He is like a tree planted by
streams of water, that yields its fruit in its season, and its leaf does
not wither. In all that he does, he prospers.*

Psalm 1:1–3 RSV

Take Time to Appreciate God's Blessings

Blessings are all around us.
If we look we can recognize a blessing in
each day, each hour, each minute,
each family member, each friend, each neighbor,
each community, each city, each nation,
each challenge, each word of encouragement,
each flower, each sunbeam, each raindrop,
each awesome wonder crafted by God,
each star, each sea, each bird, each tree,
each sorrow, each disappointment,
each faith, each prayer.

The list is endless and so are the blessings which God has bestowed upon us. Train yourself to recognize and appreciate the many blessings in your life.

V.J.R.

Blessed be your glorious name, and may it be exalted above all blessing and praise. You alone are the Lord. You made the heavens, even the highest heavens, and all their starry host, the earth and all that is on it, the seas and all that is in them. You give life to everything, and the multitudes of heaven worship you.

Nehemiah 9:5–6 NIV

Thanks for the Blessings

When I count my blessings,
   I count my fans as one,
For without fans and friends,
   the writing I have done
Would lose all its meaning,
   its warmth, and its sincereness,
For how could I write
   without feeling a nearness
To all the dear people
   who interpret each line
With their own love and kindness,
   which become part of mine.
So, more than you know,
   I thank God up above
For fans, friends, and family
   and their gifts of love.

H.S.R.

The blessing of the Lord makes rich, and he adds no sorrow with it.
Proverbs 10:22 RSV